BOY SINGING TO CATTLE

MARK D. HART

Boy Singing to Cattle

WINNER OF THE
23rd ANNUAL PEARL POETRY PRIZE
selected by ANDREA CARTER BROWN

Pearl
Editions
LONG BEACH, CALIFORNIA

Library of Congress Control Number: 2012950154

ISBN 978-1-888219-41-8

Book design by Marilyn Johnson
Cover photo: "Black Cloud Palouse" by Christal Steele © 2008

This publisher is a proud member of

[c l m p]

COUNCIL OF LITERARY MAGAZINES & PRESSES
w w w . c l m p . o r g

PEARL EDITIONS
3030 E. Second Street
Long Beach, California 90803

www.pearlmag.com

For my father,
Lt. Col. Donald C. Hart, USAF,
wheat farmer of the Palouse
1923-2003

Acknowledgments

I am grateful to the editors of the following publications, in which these poems first appeared:

Atlanta Review: "The Fellowship of the Apple"
The Berkshire Review: "North of Nauset Light Beach"
Common Ground: "Wild Turkeys"
Edgz: "Midnight in a Pond in Lincoln, Massachusetts"
Emrys: "Cattails"
Insight: "For a Cambodian Nun on Mother's Day"
The Kerf: "Solstice"
MARGIE: "Real Drinkers"
The Mid-America Poetry Review: "The Grave of My Father"
The Midwest Quarterly: "Planting Garlic"
Möbius: "Morning Glory"
Naugatuck River Review: "Dandelion Wine"
Poetry East: "As I Struggle to Pull the Pit from a Grocery Store Peach
            Picked Green," "Boy and Sheets," "Burying My Father,"
            "Chronic Fatigue Immune Deficiency Syndrome #1,"
            and "Hobos"
RATTLE: "The Calf in the Pantry" and "Torching the Playhouse"
Re)verb: "Old Stump"
Rock & Sling: "Holy Communion"
Runes: "Mercy"
The Spoon River Poetry Review: "Grace" and "A Conspiracy of Absence"
            (titled "Presence" when it first appeared)
Tar River Poetry: "Butchering"
War Poetry Contest, WinningWriters.com: "Pissing Under Pressure"
Windfall: "The North Pole"

I would like to express my gratitude to those individuals who supported me in my writing: four friends, Steve Braun, Tim Milnes, Michael Caldwell, and Michael Silverstone, who read and offered comments on my early writing and whose authentic and enthusiastic responses began to convince me it had some literary merit and gave me the courage to send it out; Sophie Craze, who wrote with me; the members of Carolyn Forché's poetry workshop at Under the Volcano 2008, who have continued since then to offer suggestions online, especially Michelle Gillette, who read the entire manuscript; the members of Alan Shapiro's 2009 & 2010 workshops at the Fine Arts Work Center in Provincetown (the same 10 people came two years in a row); Jim Moore, my writing tutor; Julie Graham, who loved my poetry while living and has supported my writing financially through her estate after her death; my family, that put up with me staring off into space a lot and disappearing into my office; and my parents, who, along with everything else, gave me the opportunity to grow up on a farm in the Palouse, whose graceful hills will always open the door to my soul.

CONTENTS

Part III

Part IV

Foreword

THE PALOUSE. Say the word. Roll it around in your mouth. Let it haunt you.

Until I read Mark Hart's *Boy Singing to Cattle*, the Palouse was just that to me—a word, a place name, albeit one with an inherent lyrical mystery. In his splendid first collection, Hart has brought to vivid life that place and the people in it. From the first poem, I was hooked.

Because Hart knows this world from the inside out, but also because he has lived with this knowledge and thought about it well into adulthood, he writes about it without sentimentality. His descriptions galvanize, yet always with a light, deft touch. Natural line breaks effectively slow down absorption to make each detail carry its full, unique weight. The recurring vocabulary of faith, often in surprising contexts, reminds the reader of the sacred that is the everyday, the routine, the here and now.

Hart brings into his portrait the geologic and human history of the area. He follows the river which both feeds and drains the Palouse. He sends the region outward in the holds of ships transporting grain across the Pacific. He connects the character of his father, a World War II veteran who survived the crash of his plane, to the risks of farming the land and his improbable survival of a second terrible accident. He notes, he celebrates, the role of alcohol in cementing the bonds of a community, in dealing with physical pain, in providing relief from grief. For it is a difficult life, one which takes its toll on the community and on the relationships between members of that community.

Boy Singing to Cattle is about the world of men. It is about the world of boys who go on to become men. It is ultimately an exploration of what it means to be a man.

This is the story of a son out of sync with his complicated, difficult father, the story of this same son, grown up, who comes to an appreciation of his father's legacy only later in his own adult life with his father's decline and death. Hart's poems about the rural life of New England which close the collection complete the cycle of an adult coming to terms with his past. When Hart describes the difficult physical labor of preparing an over-grown New England pasture for his daughter's new horse, we have come full circle. We are at once that long-ago and far-away child observing the labor which made his life possible. And the adult son, who sees himself re-enacting the rituals of his father's life and that of the community which made him. This is reconciliation at its most profound, at its most generous.

Boy Singing to Cattle is at once a moving elegy for a lost parent, a portrait of a way of life, and of the landscape and community tied to it, and a reconciliation with that past. It is remarkable for its wisdom, for the generosity of its spirit. These poems continue to haunt me—in their grittiness, their loveliness, their eloquence; for the heart which informs every poem. *Boy Singing to Cattle* renews and refreshes the tradition of poetry about the land and those who live from it in ways I would not have thought possible in the 21st century. These poems grow on you, live in you, and make you live in your own life with greater consciousness and greater forgiveness.

—Andrea Carter Brown
Los Angeles, California
December, 2012

PART I

Burying My Father

Your body lies beneath my hand,
a cold stone.

You look good. Better than
when dying perhaps, but fixed
like a photograph fresh from a chemical bath.
What kind of death in people
makes them love this
preservation?

I want to drag you
out of that box by your armpits,
throw you in the back of the car and
bury you in the garden like a dead cat,
nothing between you and the raw soil you tilled,
billions of hungry mouths ready
to eat you out of the limits of your skin,
guts exploding with gases like a newborn star,
the grass by the fence row
sparkling with spring rain,
waving in the wind,
roots reaching softly down
into your corpse
to resurrect it.

REAL DRINKERS

There was party drinking, holiday drinking,
marriage drinking, funeral drinking,
card-playing drinking, been working too hard drinking,
bad weather ruining the crops drinking, and
let's have a drink drinking.

Voices and laughter filled the house as the bottles drained,
a small Manhattan skyline on the counter,
Dad at the bar, or me as a teen, mastering
the mixology portion of his universe.
The shot glass rested unused on the shelf.
Real drinkers, Dad said,
never added pop or anything sweet.

We were not alcoholics. We were Catholics.
We had a religion to uphold in the face of
Bible Christians and Mormons sobering the West.
Dad's gospel: Never take yourself too seriously.

Straight, it burned like a foretaste of hell.
On the rocks, it jingled. Each sip
poured amber waves of grain alcohol over the brain
until it floated, edges melting. Whiskey,
the great smoother-overer and sociablizer
produced states called snockered and soused,
one S-sound after another sliding toward
sex and sleep. Maybe sin or cirrhosis.
But never stumbling or shitfaced.
Real drinkers held their liquor.

The real drinker's etiquette:
Offer refills quickly. Nudge, but never insist.
Look the other in the eye when you toast—
let life distill to two people meeting,
poised on the rim of oblivion.

With a flat clink of the glass,
the straight shot of his eyes meeting yours,
my father would say
Here's lookin' at ya.

GRACE

I'm staring at the head of a stranger,
some guy in line for coffee in front of me,
young, maybe in college,
the swirl of his hair a perfect galaxy unfolding,
a vortex that draws me in
smitten like a mother, lost in the rapture of
that precise tint and curl and pattern,
a wheel set in motion
when his father's starting-gun explosion
sent the winning helix through the gate,
the resulting head that crowned, wet and conical,
in the canyon of his mother's thighs
ejected from its sack of dreams.
Through this rose window I gaze
standing in a hallowed place until
he turns from the counter leaning into his day
and I must look down,
pretend to count my change,
do what I can
not to weep.

Butchering

The hoisted bulk of
cattle carcasses dangling cold from rafters
above the heads of sleeping trucks and tractors,
and my father on a ladder with a saw
carving off a quarter, letting it down slowly
onto his partner's shoulders
who'd stagger under its weight to the shop—
I never saw the blast to the temple,
the gutting, or the skinning,
but the naked sight of so much red muscle
shrink-wrapped in clear fascia
and packed in a white glut of fat
dropped its own dead weight
on a boy's shoulders.

I think of those cattle winter mornings
standing on new snow in pale sunlight,
spouts of breath issuing white from nostrils.

The day after Thanksgiving
in the shop where power tools
spoke aggressively to wood and metal,
commanding insubordinate matter to their master's will,
the clan would gather
and stuff the belly of the woodstove,
raising its metabolism to beat back November
reaching in through single panes,
unsealed doors and corrugated tin. The men
would stand huddled around the band saw conferring,
knowing how a piece of know-how
can stray like an animal.

Probing for joints and counting ribs
in the arcane mathematics of roasts and steaks,
they put asunder what God hath joined.
Abuzz at their own tables
knife-wielding women
would sit trimming and wrapping and labeling,
the harvest of beef flowing from their hands
into boxes for each family,
hands that had handled a lot of meat,
bodies that had sprouted other bodies,
split and opened.

My job: shoving scraps with a wooden mallet
down the grinder's gargling throat,
fingers lifting and dropping cold meat,
feet stranded on the heat-sucking concrete,
the last ruins of these
well-buttressed cathedrals of bone
a trackless heap in a stainless-steel bowl.

> On the ground bleeding
> after the wheel tractor had righted itself
> and his partner drove away for help,
> my father lay with both hips broken off from his spine and
> split up the middle to his navel.
> The tire had grabbed one foot and pulled it under
> as he tried to jump,
> the other foot caught on the machine.
> He held himself together with his cowhide belt
> and waited.
>
> He survived.
>
> I still keep that belt.

Out into the early dark and a dinner of
fresh beef, the freezer humming in the cellar
plump with white packages snug on the shelves,
the unused bone and gristle buried or left
atop the frozen ground in some far corner of the field.

In bed at night awake
the distant coyote call to prayer,
the bone-white moon.

One morning after butchering I walked
into the back fields on a fresh skiff of snow.
Paw prints converged, the bones were gone,

and the remaining herd shuffled head-down
into winter.

The Washhouse

It sidled up against the woodshop behind the house,
a weary architectural afterthought,
unheated, interior dark with barn-boards,
flies eternally buzzing to be free,
one cobwebbed window gazing outward
to a gentle curve of hillside dense with grain
like a supine goddess.

I loved that place.
No scrubbed porcelain and polished chrome.
Exposed plumbing ran through bare studs.
A few washtubs hung on the walls.
Cock-eyed floor aslant.
In the corner, a square, concrete slab,
repoured to reach the drain when the building sank,
grooved by the incontinent drip of the shower head,
a plain, plastic curtain to keep in the splash.

A long, chipped sink screwed to the wall.
Just a tiny mirror to frame the head,
the whole washhouse a mirror,
an unkempt sanctuary
housing men unclothed and unashamed,
their sun-shy regions in the half-light
pale like roots pulled from the ground.

Red enameled wheel-spokes on the hot knob,
naked gray spokes on the cold—
I liked to grip the pipe until it grew too hot,
feel the cold pipe grow colder as the spring water entered.

A bare bulb on a pull-string
lit late after-harvest showers,
dinner waiting.

And drying after, if last in line, lingering
in the joyous gap of clean but not yet clothed,
alone with the steam.

The Grave of My Father

I must place with you,
like King Tutankhamen in his tomb,
the things you will need in the afterlife
to know who you are: a deck of cards,
some whiskey, a pocket knife, bailing wire
and duct tape—there must be duct tape—
some stocks to trade, a picture book
about The War. You are a simple man.
You do not need jewels or robe.
But a wife would be handy, I think,
to tell you how to dress, to tell you
what to do, someone to resist.
And someone not your wife
to flirt with. I'm not sure how
I'll get them in. These things
don't go over well these days,
you know. I would place in there
the open sky, packets of seeds,
and lots of loam. Well, I guess
the last you will not need, for you
are lying in it. Nor the sky,
for it is always with you in the blue
of your eyes. With these few things
I know you will be comfortable
and not too lost or at loose ends
in the fields of the beyond.

Morning Glory

My father couldn't kill it. Settlers
spread west with their desperate hope
invasive seed no native could repel.

It leapt from garden plots and now
grows wagon circles of green
on the wheat field's blond stubble.

They say its roots reach thirty feet below.
Commit herbicide on this intruder and it wilts
but rises from the earth anew to greet you
with a vining lilt and flowery brogue.

* * *

My father couldn't stop the magpies either,
winged rabble in the cottonwoods at dawn
talking trash, squawking their ugly squawk.

He kept a loaded shotgun in the bedroom,
window open. Summer mornings
we might wake to the glory of that blast

then lie in the cool stillness of the house,
the scent of dew on wheat straw wafting
through open windows, the first tint of sun
blooming pink on the granary's tin siding.

* * *

Soon the birds, wary scouts, would beat it
at the first poking out of barreled snout.
Then curses flew at breakfast too.

Once my father snuck out the backdoor,
blew one pesky magpie off a fence post.
But the thrill of his triumph was short.

Behind the post stood the chicken house,
walls riddled with shot,
vacant panes staring back at him
in the uncommonly still twilight.

GETTING THE CALL

After the phone call, silence.
Your cousin who had
farmed with you for forty years
had been there feeding you
spoon by spoon, your eyes shut.
In the pause before dessert
your lips turned pale. Gone—
a heron lifting off the pond.
Your eyes, Mom said,
had been a brilliant blue today.
Perhaps you saw the open sky before you
beckoning all day.
I take refuge in the garden,
drink a toast to you
under a whiskey-colored moon,
Here's lookin' at ya, Dad,
watch you hoe the corn and beans,
the air once more full of dust and sun,
hear you tell me, yet again, how
any job I can get that pays
more than two bucks an hour
beats growing vegetables. Yet
you grew a garden every year.
I do too—to hoe and plant and watch things grow,
to be close to you and something you knew,
never spoken, I had tasted in the dust
by your side. Farmer and pilot,
you knew the earth and sky and
the tension between them.

How oddly right
to make love with my wife tonight
while you grow cold,
to join this ending to its inexplicable beginning,
you still here
in the quickening of my body.

THE CALF IN THE PANTRY

At the base of cream-colored cabinets,
the milk of his newborn face
gazing toward the kitchen,
the brown rug of his body
shivering on the linoleum, unlicked,
slick with the balm of his intrauterine life,
the abandoned calf, legs bent and
untried beneath him, lay at the feet
of the very utility sink where,
after the fall butchering,
cold cow hearts
would be soaking in a pail.

I imagined Dad in coveralls
carrying the calf in his arms from the barnyard
just like the plaster shepherd
in the Christmas crèche.

We kids dabbed him dry with towels,
eager for the feel of him. We mixed
warm water with formula and fed him
from a bucket with a huge latex nipple
protruding from its side, his throat
greedily sucking and swallowing.
All the while, a rose bush behind the house
scratched on the window pane
buffeted by a cold March wind.

THE VANISHING POINT

I.

At the crossroads of corridors by the nurses' station
you slouch in your wheelchair,
swallowed by sleep.
                    I shake you
and you suck the air to straighten up,
eyes void, expression flatlined,
walls, ceiling, floor receding blank behind you
meeting at infinity.

II.

                    The week of my stay,
ladies in billowing clouds of white and wispy hair
taxi on the runway for clearance, old men
sink into themselves like jack-o-lanterns
a week past Halloween,
                    but you sit stiff,
a mannequin the nurses have dressed and molded.
The buried shunt, snake of plastic tube
beneath your skin from skull to chest
implanted to relieve the pressure on your brain
at first drained your mind—
                    Uncle Harry,
dead for 30 years, comes to visit you,
your son-in-law flies a plane and parks it at your door—
but then words followed sense down the serpentine drain.
        Now you sit in silence,
eyes often closed, as if seeing takes too much,
sometimes staring at the tray,
juicy fruit, sweet frosting you desire,
and I jump, buck private to your order,

waiting for some sign of your will.
When done, you simply do not
open for the spoon.

You rarely move. Only neck and jaw and eyes
keep their animal birthright of motion.
I massage your shoulders
once again the boy behind you
in the chair that neither kid nor cat dare claim,
combing your hair while you watch TV.
Only once do I see you move your arm.
A pretty nurse comes in and breaks the spell.
You reach for her hand, less by intention perhaps than by
a reflex running down its well-trod neural path,
and in that gesture I feel a lifetime
of wishing you would reach for me.

III.

Your breathing, the room,
its off-white walls and metal bed,
artifacts of your life stuck on walls—the you
fully haired and hormoned,
in your P-51,
          three swastikas proudly painted on the rim of the cockpit,
faces of the brood who resemble you in name and form,
                    and framed by the window,
the hills of the Palouse where you farmed for 40 years—
it is all growing still, this life,
one breath at a time,
contained in four walls not your own,
and a body
turning to stone.

And yet it seems for years at home
you had practiced being mute and frozen,
sinking ever lower in your chair,
hiding in your earphones and TV,
ever less a presence—

                         vanishing before our eyes.

You named me for a general,
tried to make me tough,
filleting this heart
on the edge of what you called humor:
Mark'll make a good wife someday.
Were you ashamed of me?
Under your command, Colonel, I have learned
what I know about silence and turning to stone
but of late I have wished again to be flesh.

IV.

A good day comes toward the end of my stay
when the blue of your eyes meet mine. I speak
of frozen mornings donning rubber boots and overalls
to kick broken bales of hay off the bed of the old Dodge
idling driverless in compound low along the flat,
hungry hordes of cattle plodding behind,
snorting steam, plopping piles,
and of summer mornings when the dune-like hills
lay soft and round in the growing light
sweet with the smell of dew,
of oven-baked, dusty afternoons,
vast spaces, dry

                   and open to the sky,
the drone of the combine,
the swat of a cow's tail.

I thank you
for giving me this land,
the rapture of her ever-changing moods,
the dirt, the dust, the mud,
the greening, gilding, then final browning of it,
a rich life, the inner landscape I inhabit,
with you there, almost grown from earth itself,
its keeper, prodding it to yield its fruit.
And while I speak this litany
you look at me.
I cannot know if you understand.
I cannot see behind those eyes.
But when I end *I love you, Dad*
you lurch
and say *I love you too.*

Four words.
Four words, so quickly out—
were they a reflex
following my cue? Yet—you never
lurched to answer *how are you?* Had you
heard it all? Had you
come from your own vanishing
to reach for me?

V.

The next day, my last day,
the plane for Boston waiting,
your eyes closed, exhausted, I feed you
locked within your browning senses.
I open the curtains,
closed to better see the tube,
let the sun blaze bright wings across the wall.

With a freedom born of nothing left to say or do
released from your command, I weep.
           You raise your lids,
like pulling the cord of a heavy blind,
and look upon me crying,
tears calling you from your stupor,
release on me this one last time
the blue of your sky.

Then fatigue takes you.

I sit and sit and stare at you,
this my final look,
                        stand to walk,
and look again—your thin hair, almost white,
the pigment patches on your scalp,
your whiskers flecked with gray,
the hair on your arms.
I walk toward the door, turn—
your apartment in limbo,
you sunk in rest, breathing,
your head from behind,
slightly to one side.

Cattails

All day long
I have been coaxing my silence to speak,
but it only looks on,
      animal, mute,
            awake,

and I envy the eloquence of cattails
      whose clatter
punctuates the wind's long phrases
leaving the landscape
      more silent.

FLIGHT FROM DUXFORD

Laughter, smoke, the triumph of
your luck last night at poker
fade behind you with the hedged fields
of England, and, in your chariot of steel
sheering the wind, humming
its hymn of glory—a constant drone
beside your brothers—you gaze
over clouds to that blue yonder
and an ever-receding rim of earth.
You peer down into passing chasms
to the gray furrows of the North Sea.
Alone in your cockpit, there is only
the vast morning of your youth
and the trip before you. Not long ago
you were riveting at Boeing;
now a P-51 bears you, buoyed
by the invisible.

              But flying back
a sudden cavity in sound,
an eerie whisper of air enshrouds
your fuselage—that class you skipped,
the one that taught you how your
life raft inflates, matters now
three miles off the coast of Holland,
hydraulics bleeding, hit by flack
or the blast of your own bombs,
your prop stopped, and the sea
rising to meet you. At 1000 feet you bail:
One short swing and I was in the water.
I had almost figured it too close.

Just floating, embraced by the sea,
brine like blood in your mouth.
Above, your buddy marks you
with carrion circles, eyes on the gas gauge
while your vital heat drains.
You see your mother coming to the door,
the telegram, the wave of the news
taking her down. There is a
great tenderness where all things touch,
where the puny will is weightless.
And a strength. You shear the valve
bare handed, the rescue launch reports,
reaching you hanging on, half-inflated.
Why did you survive?

                              Never a report
of your thoughts 30 years later
when the tractor tipped you off,
split you open between the legs,
and left you in the summer fallow
staring upward at that constant blue,
gauging your luck. A partner there,
again, a witness who got help,
and you lived another 28 years,
hips bolted onto the spine, a colostomy,
a sphincter transplant that leaked,
done in finally at 80 by drowning
in the fluid of your own brain.
Suspended from two towers of grace,
the span of your life hung.
Where are you now, O twice survivor?
Give me your altitude and velocity.
The clouds here have condensed,
rained, and slowly vanish into air.

Tassels of the unmowed grass
beside the roadway grasp the last
few rays of sunlight and hold them,
waving them before my eyes,
and long contrails to somewhere
stretch across heaven.

The North Pole

Here snowdrifts melt last, the road
back of our land cuts into a north hillside
too steep to farm we call "The North Pole."
From the hilltop, highest point around,
you look east across wheat fields into Idaho,
the dark, pine-covered distance.

Wind carved these hills. They roll
like cresting waves toward that blue-green shore,
giant sea swells of green in spring,
gold late summer.
Sit patiently at dusk and
wildlife appears—deer, badger, skunks, rabbits—
shy offspring of the land.
Up here there's almost always wind
rustling the grass, drumming the ears,
a sweet solitude in those sounds
constant as surf.

I come here to be alone, the world beneath me,
to sit in the lap of its vast expanse,
in a home without walls,
where I gaze into another state.

I return as I must to this spot,
the sun's cathedral arch spanning dawn to dusk,
the earth conversing with a moody sky,
this still point around which my 50 years have turned,
the North Pole,
where the compass points within.

As I Struggle to Pull the Pit from a Grocery Store Peach Picked Too Green

I think of the orchards of Penawawa in my youth
before the dams, when the Snake still ran free,
how, in the deep canyon—mild, protected—
peach trees thrived, and the flats along the river
swelled with them. Late in the summer
we'd pick as a family for canning;
on a branch in a bower of leaves,
I could eat peach after ripe peach.
Ancient hunters had made winter camps here,
and we sifted the riverbank for arrowheads;
the chipped, translucent obsidian when washed
glinted like a swift-flowing stream.
I think of the view from the top of the grade,
the long, hot trip down the serpentine road,
hills and gullies brown with dried-up grasses,
and, at the bottom, coming ever nearer,
the river bend,
                    its oasis of green.

My Father's Farm

A whiff of baking bread— Following the nose,
I'm bound for the kitchen, stomach empty
in its hip-held bowl beneath my clothes,
robust hunger in me rising like that cresting
amber crust in oven's womb I'll soon slice
and smear with butter, grateful for those,
knuckles creased with flour, who knead and roll,
or, knuckles creased with dirt, who reap and sow.

On my father's farm, hills stand like loaves
at harvest time, their gold flows in augered streams
out the spouts of green combines—every kernel,
hard and keen, bound for the digestive tract
of animal or human being. My father's wheat
passes daily through this world in pipes of flesh
and pipes of clay and steel away from every meal
to meet again the earth from which it grew.

My father sows the sprout to raise the waving stalk
and serves up yet another crop upon these
dunes of once volcanic dust, now loam.
The day her rumblings turned to roar, St. Helen's
spewed an inch of soot upon this home. I heard
a pop of distant shotgun in Seattle when she blew
and knew the ancient alchemy of elements to aliments,
how crust of earth would turn to crust of bread.

Shipped out the mouth of the Columbia to mouths
of Yokohama workers slurping steaming *udon* from bowls
or, in Shanghai, piling tangled heaps of yellow *mee-yun*,
people crave my father's gold to pay the creditor

who beats daily on the belly door. Hunger's
cresting waves pile ceaselessly upon their shore.
Six billion bellies make an awesome thunder rumbling.
They wake a man at night if he has ears to hear.

Bound for lands of Morning Calm and Rising Sun,
aboard the rolling pitch of ship, within the hollow hold,
westward in an arrowed wave steams my father's gold.
Atop a blue-green rim of earth full circle round,
a blue-green marble swirled with white, it rolls
beneath a red ball rising, melting night. Silently
earth rolls upon its tether swung around a yellow star—
bound to one another as all bodies are.

The Field

I see you as a charged particle
emerging in a quantum field,
sunlight glaring off your bald head
not nearly as round as the physicist's atom.

You are standing in a wheat field—your field—
whose golden waves, transparent as flame,
extend infinitely, the magnetic field
formed of your intention.

People reach into that plenum to find their bread,
they stand with you in that field that feeds them,
millions, oblivious to you and it,
the field that calls the farmer to it.

I grow up in that field, another particle
emerging from indivisible being,
remaining a while in its fullness,
a boy playing in the dirt, building roads,

sailing in a divine wind of indeterminacy
until your gaze fixes me in time and space,
sees me as deficient—too sensitive,
awkward with tools, afraid of you,

angry. Particles out of phase,
we perturb each other. I drive the truck,
follow the combine around,
haul grain to town. I circle you.

I leave. Though far away working
in my own field I am imprinted by that wave,
it localizes me wherever I go.
I can never really leave.

I furrow the page, like you I feed
the hungry who seek to eat
from that fullness in which we stand,
indivisible, yet as particles apart.

You discharge your charge and I look again
and you are not, the particle now
gone from the field that called it.
Yet the waves of your having been

do not stop,
can never stop.
They call me now
to speak of our home.

DUSK IN THE PALOUSE

The thin, semi-desert air
gives up the heat of summer swiftly.
Like stepping away from a campfire,
a chill meets you, and with it
the sweet, fertile smell
of wheat straw growing damp,
erotic in the folds of the hills
slipping into darkness. Sounds
begin to carry as on water through the still air,
a voice across the highway by some acoustic magic
speaks quietly in the ear, and one by one
stars appear in the auditorium of heaven
like people seating themselves for a show.
Standing outside, looking into the lit house,
to that world oblivious to dusk, lost
in its whisky glow and conversation,
standing in the cool twilight
growing darker as the day flees west,
soft curves of silhouetted hills fading,
pores in the earth sweating dew,
you hear the tall grain stir and whisper
come away from the human
and be of the earth, of the dusk,
of the silence waiting to the heard,
go into the venereal hills,
at home in the house of night.

PART II

BOY SINGING TO CATTLE

Their white Hereford faces
face the white boards
and the boy beyond,
eyes steady, ears cupped
to drink at this pure source
singing from a deep well inside him
tender for their trust
and curious to touch.

His voice without command
opens a gate
they move toward.

Not the mothers,
face down in their all-consuming grind,
only the calves, one hoof at a time,
push back the frontier of instinct
to come toward the human
who charms their simple, beastly hearts
closer by degrees to that patient hand
outstretched across the fence.

His slightest touch
wakes ancestral fear—
they bolt, scatter,
turn, wait, listen,
begin again this slow wave
toward the shore of their
primal, bovine sea and a star
suddenly brighter in their darkness.

Holy Communion

He spent one June head bowed
staring down from a timbered bridge
into still water mirroring blue.
From under the slender arching grass,
the wet, brown stone
of a muskrat's head
arrowed grooves in that glass
and buckled a bladed sky.

Here was a quiet kingdom,
well-contained, a heaven on earth
of succulent roots and silken mud
where the brushed grass quaked
from her broad behind
and she preached her silent sermon
of simple grace, a creature in her place
gliding from bank to tufted bank.

She was his secret life
beside the clutter of rooms,
the clatter of his kind,
and he knew the spot
where she entered
her cottage beneath the sod,
he knew the two that followed her
to their nest in that womb of earth.

The meek shall inherit
cool water, green fields
stroked by the breeze—

On a pew of creosote boards he sat
dangling his bare feet down
and partook of her holy communion
where air and earth come together
with a rippling flow between.

In the Closet

Limp, soft, unoccupied—
his parents' clothes
at his perusal.
                    The waft of a blouse,
his nails bouncing backward over tight
furrows of corduroy or stroking
the smooth length of a tie.
He has license to finger or fill them,
or simply lie on a bed of shoes,
breathless forms floating
                    weightlessly above.
He likes to gather a bunch together and
inhale through the thick lot of them,
taking their combined essence
into himself.

They did not heed his pleas
and left, but here
the animal musk of them stays,
and he burrows in.

COW PATHS

Ever crossing trails
traverse the hillside,
and they roam upward
without a goal in mind,
boys up to their waist
in wide summer, who
only know the next thing
when they find it.

Unobstructed blue,
open ground,
the strange paths
creatures have taken
to be a body in this world—
a groundhog, a rabbit,
a sky-riding hawk,
a pheasant exploding to flight,
a mouse the hawk seizes,
and a bull snake in the grass
that rears up like a cobra.

A question runs on ahead—
where is the herd?
Probably plopped in the
shade of the Ponderosas
lazing after their morning graze.

Boys at War

Dirt clods detonate
against the dirt clod rampart
they crouch behind,
but they keep on popping up
to lob back more of those
brown nuggets of glee.

A truce—one removes
a speck from his brother's eye.

Abandoning field for tree,
they ride a timbered ship
across a grassy sea.
Yarh! There's sure to be treasure
buried in the weeds out back.
But first, a hostage to kidnap—
the cat must walk the plank.

They die with gusto,
grab their hearts and fall
quickened to stand again
without a judgment day
or trumpet call.

What puts the war into
a boy's heart? And what
could possibly take it out?
They come in for a snack
with a whoop and a shout.

Boy and Sheets

Hanging on the line,
the snap of the wind
put the freshness in them,
then the dampness,
left out too late into dusk.

He put the dirt in them,
blood from cuts and
bug bites he scratched,
dead skin peeled from sunburn,
a faint scent of cocoa butter.

The cat put the cat hair,
the fleas, the claw holes
of rapturous kneading in them
as the boy stroked him
before falling asleep.

Dreams slipped the ghosts
of his day in them,
undrinkable potions
he drank anyway, clouds
in his vast, invisible sky.

PART III

The Fellowship of the Apple

I.

Unlike grafted apples,
those factories and suburban tracts of taste,
pippins, with a name as mischievous and sprightly as any,
are wildlings sprung from apples mating freely.
Rampant with heterozygosity—
color ranging from white to nearly black,
size from nickels to grapefruit,
habit from columnar to sprawling—
in them long-dead languages of apple speak in new tongues,
sour, bitter, mealy, rarely sweet,
with undertones of flavor as complex
as a human heart.
Multiform the face,
cacophonous the voice
of apple.

II.

Down from the village church,
behind the clapboard farmhouse—the orchard,
a leafy choir raising a silent hymn to Bacchus
in these vineyards of the 19th century north.
Come autumn, men in sheds like amorous schoolboys
plied their art and opened the sense-pores,
breathing the sweet apple essence bursting from skins—
the gush into mash, the run
sloshing with singular purpose into the frank pales,
pale amber gallons in glass,
the twinkle, the tang, the froth,
the blessed deliverance of cider.

III.

As a student in Austria,
in the company of Austrians,
on a pilgrimage to a church on a road
winding upwards through fields, woods,
and mountains after mountains,
we'd pause at farmhouses asking for water, knowing
would come instead a sour *Apfulmost*
and a lively, red-skinned farmer tart with humor
wielding his wildling dialect words.
Cider, chocolate, schnapps, espresso beans
to chew, raw smoked bacon, hearty bread
multiplied like loaves and fishes,
and, filled with these holy spirits,
we'd set forth again singing, looking for more God
to have on the way to the church,
growing ever more fond of each other
in the fellowship of the apple.

TORCHING THE PLAYHOUSE

It had been an old pig barn, and
we squealed to have it as our own, mopped it out,
washed the windows, dragged into it desks, chairs,
and a couch resembling Freud's that now
lights into smoke and flame and
vanishes like a dream.
Labs with colored chemicals whose jars
beckoned like crayons to idle minds exploring a
Middle Earth between innocence and adulthood
fall and shatter as tables and shelves
give way beneath them. Posters, calendars,
remnants of the haunted house for Halloween
flower into flame, we watch them go,
watch flames lick the rough boards, hungry,
inside because we lit the match
until heat drives us out and we stand back
bright-eyed, flames crawling from rafters,
scrambling up the roof, leaping off the ridge,
roaring, bestial, eating out the blackening core
more swiftly than we had guessed.
Arsonists of our childhood,
privy to the plans to burn it anyway,
we seize the chance to fire this final rocket,
to send something of our intensity skyward,
adrenal, no hope of recovery, we want to see
the deep death latent in all things, play with it,
welcome it, fill our ignorance of it,
let the structure collapse
and its matter and time implode into
the black holes of our eyes.

MIDNIGHT IN A POND
IN LINCOLN, MASSACHUSETTS

Non recte recipit haec nos rerum natura nisi nudos

—Pliny

The fluid warmth of woman
        entered as a sacrament,
    the pond takes the body in
    and floats the mind within the senses
        with the timeless ease of dreams.
This night,
this dark of humid, moonless night,
        this lover close
    whispers of splash and slosh and breath,
    ripples down the belly line,
        long smooth flow propelled off feet,
            long sweep of night ahead.
Sinking softly
        through the black sheen—
unbroken contact,
    no light, no weight, no sound, no thought,
        no place like this
            outside the womb.

Paddling on my back,
        the dome of stars above,
    thoughts of lost Odysseus,
    this speckled map and guile his only guide to home
        and mine to where I entered,
            but drifting thoughts
    have but quick suck,
    for the flesh islands are under siege by bugs.
        I stroke my breast and duck my head
            to the starless shadows of shore.

Ankle deep and climbing out
               a click
I am blasted—a blinding flash—
           pale skin in neon.
He asks me, yes,
            to put my hands above my head
       (lest I grab for gun—or towel?)
       in a drama staged for crickets,
            full frontal illumination—he says
                       It's unsafe to swim alone at night.
            Had he ever done the same?
Something about a uniform and badge and bugs
does not invite the asking
           and speeds me to the tattletale car,
the jolt not unlike the time
           a resident of this wealthy town
complained to me the trails bring in
the *hoi polloi* from Boston.
           I, in dirty T-shirt and jeans
                was building the trail as a summer job,
               struggling evenings (no kidding)
                   with Attic Greek.

Let her pull her blanket of money
           up tight around her neck,
      let her guard the night against the riff-raff
      with the officer as her fence.
I, the intruder,
           shall rise from real scum
      wet with unrepentant joy,
      exposed but not ashamed to wear
           the only uniform issued to us all,
               alive with risk and pleasure,
           and brush against the edgeless edge
               of Eden.

Dandelion Wine

Some objected to my barnyard source.
But so many grew there, such excess,
smiling.

Still smiling in the bucket, brimming,
effervescent, resinous—
the color of heaven.

Nothing in the house spoke this language.
I'd stare at my face in the mirror—
Where is it, the bright bloom?

Fingers stained with saffron, "butter"
we'd once smeared in faces, I uproot
the fine filaments for hours.

Sugar, yeast. Blond raisins for body.
A week of frothing madness in the pantry,
Dionysian vapors overwhelming every room,
then a month in jars under airlock
in the cool of the root cellar, in the dark,
in the dirty underbelly of the house,
bubbling.

Science: A few grains of sugar
made it bloom in the bottle, too much
made a bomb.

I was eighteen.

We drank it young. It was fragrant.
A hint of yellow caught the light.

PISSING UNDER PRESSURE

A friend told me once, laughing of course,
of the terror of Fenway Park—a long, tin trough
in the men's room, now extinct, whose thunder
would measure the force of a man's instinct.
There on the brink of this gaping oracle he'd stand,
self in hand,
                    awaiting its chorus,
long in his place with a line behind
in a deafening silence,
soaked in disgrace.

              In that moment of pressure
the mind strips you bare, unconscious exposed
to a jury of strangers, eyes to the wall,
standing it seems for men everywhere.
How do you compare?
                       You seize at the root.
You stare and you stare, flag unfurled,
till you leave the stand, case closed,
condemned to sit in a stall—
girled.

      For boisterous boys outdoors
unzip drawers in plain view with a feral joy,
burn names in snow, force this icy foe
to retreat in the face of their youthful heat
and run away yellow.
        And musketeers after too many beers
cram shoulder to shoulder in a barroom stall
for a bet, draw swords *All for one and one for all!*
to strike in sync at the common pot. Why not?

In their jostle and jeers, camaraderie rules,
each showing his membership card
to this club of fools.
    So men, we're told, are supposed to be,
to spill into life in this jocular way, be bold,
aim at the bowl of some corporate goal,
make the gold stream flow,
write their names in snow.

        But for some, it's not easy
to come ungripped. It's not for me—
I was there, you see, unzipped
in the john, and my sword
didn't flash. Instead, tight-lipped, I was gored
in a good-natured crossfire, a loser of bets,
but sore from a wound that had come long before:
unathletic, quick to tears,
girled on the schoolyard, teased
for a temper I could not contain,
I heard one day as a teen said in disdain
of another,
        Can't piss under pressure,
and the phrase grew below in the very place
where a father's red face at his awkward son
and the bruises and welts of words can be found
till a new fear blossomed on
shame's fertile ground.

        Now this one, shy muscle,
this oracle of flesh, not of tin,
will speak its silence in the unspoken discourse of men
with a rattling flood of unruly rhyme.

Are you listening, you men, who stand at the wall?
Can you read what is written in angry scrawl?
I'm making it plain:
                    Piss on you all
who feel so entitled to make others
feel small!

                    I'm shocked that you're shocked
when men (and women) in arms act in roles they've rehearsed
and reversed since age three:
                              On a hard prison floor,
unkindness's stage, prisoners strip themselves bare
to the officers' glee, who, convinced of their liberty,
write names on each page with an ink you can't see.
(Then use photography!) Down under
where men at birth are sewn tight
these surgeons open a slit in the seam,
slip the bastard seed of their cruelty between.
Rammed from behind, up through their pride,
a cartridge of rage explodes in each mind,
lips forming a silent vow—not knowing how—
to blow the dread-cage of this heart apart,
make the floor like a face
flush with red.

                    How does a man know his true worth?
By length or by girth? Who's on top, who's the best,
who's first? Who can humiliate whom the worst?
Raw mornings I wake with a chest of ground meat,
the sinews of meaning
                          just don't connect.
I'm not alone in this plight,
I suspect.

Those mornings
I walk to the end of the pasture, I stop
where birches speak truth—white, silent, and tall—
and there I beat the deep drum of this earth.
With nothing to measure but knowing the sum,
I give it my flavor. And the light's soft gleam
appears as a weave in a reborn umbilical stream.
Then my dog marks my scent with hers
and assures herself to her olfactory kind, *He's mine.*
Under the unjudging gaze of the sky at least
there's solace, and in these woods and the company of
this simple beast
with her jealous love.

If you come really close,
if you undo the clothes of this life,
put your palm to its very skin,
there's just this quivering pulse,
this breath. Once you burrow in,
once you've lived close and dear with that, then
fear is just fear,
and what held you back
from filling this life as you thought your right
delivers you more and more
into its tender, trembling
core.

I once watched a small boy
enjoying his nakedness under the sun
flex the bow of his brown torso and legs and
let his arrow fly, and there came this grin,
this broad, silly grin on him I found in
me as well,
the grin of a young god.

CHRONIC FATIGUE
IMMUNE DEFICIENCY SYNDROME # 1

I went for years without a diagnosis,
blood tests normal. "For someone
basically well like you" my doctor offered,
"psychotherapy could help."

A mother at my son's preschool
dismissed it. "We're *all* tired."

But the new doctor in town,
young and bearded, listened for an hour.
Fatigue, headaches, sore throats,
night sweats, aching, brain fog—
I came with symptoms listed 1 to 29

(a hypochondriac for sure). Around symptom 17

he looked up from his clipboard,
met my eye. "Wow," he said
with disarming innocence.
"You must be miserable.
How do you live like that?"

No physician ever touched me there.
I could have wept. I could have
melted to a puddle on the floor.

But some manly pride resisted.
"I have to" was all I said.

CHRONIC FATIGUE
IMMUNE DEFICIENCY SYNDROME #2

Some days I have to turn
my wedding picture to the wall:
I can't stand the sight of that
healthy guy.

Other days, before the bathroom mirror,
I stare long into weary eyes
just trying to find him.

He must be
off in some back room of the brain
resting, playing solitaire, jerking off
—who knows—
but I persist
until he appears.

Until I can exclaim
Here you are.

Until I can remind him
We're not dead yet.

Until I can whisper
I miss you.

Hobos

A few appeared when I was young,
rough as barn boards, strong as baling wire,
a remnant of the horse-days past,
looking for work and food. They ate
in the grass at the driveway's end
down the long row of cottonwoods.
My mother sent them there, away from the house.
I wandered down with my dog to see them,
these roofless men who walked out of nowhere.
They walked out of the back roads and fields
of my memory today. Why did they come?

When I bought my first house with my bride,
I dreamed a homeless man slept in the yard.
I tried to make him leave.
But he knew he belonged, unwelcome,
lest I forget.

These city bums, they don't seem the same.
I did not pity the hobos of my youth,
faces sun-tanned and lined with sorrow.
They came, hat in hands, ashamed,
and knew the dignity of shame.
They knew life owed them nothing,
and let nothing own them.

FOR A CAMBODIAN NUN ON MOTHER'S DAY

From the land of brutal slaughter,
a jungle flower uprooted and replanted
amid the granite, hemlock, maple, pine
of this New England hillside,
Ye Wan holds no tension in her eyes,
holds no sight,
just a clear space from which she smiles.

"Mahhk, you have muthah?"

The question, like she, arises out of nowhere;
conversation, it seems, but more.
Being blind, she hears the unseen.

"Yes, she lives in Washington State," I answer.

Yet I feel an orphan, a child left behind.
The world that raised me rushes off
in its mad pursuit of happiness,
while I, alone and lonely,
show up hungry at her door.

Here are but shoddy trailers.
Women, bent with age, seek their footing in the snow.
The bathroom floor sags with rot.
The shrine has plastic flowers.
The wiring makes me nervous.
Why, then, when I am here, am I so happy?

"Would you be my mother, Ye?" I think.

No need to ask.
She bore no child to be a bosom for all.
Holding the box of cookies I offer like a chest of gold,
she chants for my well-being,
and the gift, now released from self,
flows out to all that breathes.

MERCY

My throat is a clenched fire,
an arson's match. All day long I have
watched a huge porcupine
like a pile of coal or a burnt stump
move about the yard in the cold rain
eating apples, satisfying the
soft, needy underside she protects,
and I think I know what it is
to cause anguish to those who touch you,
to forage alone, and to crave
sweet mouthfuls of mercy.

PART IV

WILD TURKEYS

This voiceless land is speaking
  its mother tongue to them—
    an upturned grub, another mouthful
      merciful and sweet. I watch

the brown hulls of their bodies
  traverse a green sea,
    gleaning the meadow—preservation land.
      Forced to idle

behind a school bus,
  my daily migration to work
    interrupted, the beauty, the wildness
      preserves me

from my haste,
  I open to this unfilled space
    fog lifting from wet grass,
      a pale sun

slowly burning through, and
  for twenty seconds I am with them
    in their bellied, soft suckling on
      this breast we call earth.

OLD STUMP

Could I ever be this beautiful
after I'm dead,
luminous green with moss so soft,
patches of blue-green lichen?
The rotting wood shows through
like a grooved and eroded cliff face—
could my bones come to light
through flesh like that?
If I were left above ground undisturbed,
would a hemlock sapling
arch from my belly like a fountain?

Solstice

Squatting by the fire:
the same old skin,
same old stack of bones.

The dragon sleeping in the wood is awake
and writhes upon its jeweled hoard
stolen from a nearby star.

Many ages we have stared
into this great undoing, voyeurs
of carbon mating with molecules of air,

gazing into the secret of our very body,
this walking stove, slow burn we feed,
sometimes hearth to another,

in the flickering of memories and dreams
ever vanishing in the flames before us
sensing we are children of the one

mother light.

To Gus Johnson (in memoriam)

Angel of Wheeler Avenue,
you came with muddy boots and callused hands,
dirt pressed into the creases of the skin,
bringing a plow to get us out, a saw
to cut the storm-felled tree that blocked the road,
a truck to haul away the dear, dead horse,
or a jump on fall's first morning chilled with frost,
when you heard my pickup groan a feeble crank.
We wondered how you seemed to always know
without a call to show up at the scene.
However early I rose to have my run,
the light in the barn announced to me that you
were there already, milking, and, if you'd
look up and see me pass, your *Mo-ahnin', Mahhk*
with a Yankee lilt spanning half an octave,
rising at the end like a puppydog's tail,
never failed to lift my spirits skyward too.
A big Swede, shy, of few words but heartfelt presence,
the sort of man who'd keep two burly oxen,
who took to my Dad, wheat farmer from the west,
as a kindred soul who, like you, made a living
from the earth, you were tough and gentle, innocent
and wise, with guileless eyes soft as a child's,
the lamb of God who took away our burden
each winter-weary March, when we'd drive the roads
with trees all uddered and bucketed for the milking
and know that with the mud and gritty snow
would come that amber taste of winter's passing—
sap stored in dark and fibrous roots to rise
with waxing warmth and sun to burst the buds,

a sweet elixir that you caught and brewed,
ensconced till late inside the sugar house,
fire crackling, steam rising to the gods,
and offering hot to all your visitors
in tiny paper cups the sweetness you
extracted from the harsh New England winter.
We felt the warmth and cheer of it—and you
the slop and toil, the aching back, and so
in '91 you shipped a gallon jug
to General Schwarzkopf, to thank him for
a war well fought and countless, weary hours.

So we were shocked to learn, on Christmas Day,
that you were gone—like a favorite tree blown down.
A storm came while you were outside chopping wood.
What did you think that wintry day, as you felt
it rage inside your chest, as you looked upon
your life-long home that snuggled there amid
the stony fields, encircling woods? Did the beauty
and sorrow of this world break your heart?
You told the medics *no heroics*, for
you feared death less than incapacity,
to be idle while there was work to do, but then
at calling hours your hands as big as mitts
lay strangely idle on a breathless chest.

Your presence hangs upon this valley still
like fog when warmth of air meets cold of snow.
You were in the very fiber of the wood
I fed my stove last winter. You were slathered
on every pancake. This time of year, as kids

return to school, as mornings hold a chill,
and all is bathed in warm September light,
I think how you will not be here to bring
a load of cordwood to our door this year
or join us drinking coffee by the stove.
I was not close to you, yet close enough
to know that, like the cougar I saw last June
cross before me on the road, one such as you
is something rare to meet, something to tell of,
though you would be the last to think it so.
As I look past the beauty of the fall
toward the long and bitter cold ahead,
I'm happy to be sad today
and boil down into a poem that all may taste
the sweetness that was you.

A Conspiracy of Absence

To remember,
my wife moves her ring
to the opposite finger: on one hand
a wrongness of touch, on the other
an inconsolable absence. Nights
when we go to bed angry, my arm
not under her head nor her hand
on my chest, what unyielding pressure
that absence is, seducing from anger
an admission of loss. Tonight
as we gaze upward at stars and
the gaping darkness beyond,
we feel the lack of an answer
surrounding us.

NORTH OF NAUSET LIGHT BEACH

The grin of day upon the lip of earth,
        pink skin of dawn—
I strip to feel it, let it break upon me,
        the first faint warmth,
go down to the lap and glistening chill
        of the urgent sea
past mating waves that frothing mount,
        driven toward the shore,
out to where the feet lift groundless
        from the floor
rocked in the rhythm that first
        fathered us in this world.

Taut like rubber, black as a tire,
        snort of breath
you burst the surface before me,
        startling us both
hairless in our warm, milk-suckled flesh,
        we gawk each other,
seal and man in a rising tide
        of fear and wonder.

You here at home, I feel the sea suck
        heat from my marrow,
vast grave, devouring mother,
        yet kin, long-lost kin
I ken the snug, sure tug of moon,
        the toss of wind,
the wasted wash of love
        upon a shifting shore,
the urges of this brief life
to break and return.

Planting Garlic

I love to imagine the first blind rootings
in gravity's dark light, the sodden waiting,
the slow ignition of their tiny green rockets

as I bury their pink-skinned cheeks
in the corpse-cold ground soon freezing to stone.
My neighbor says the mounded beds look like

freshly dug graves. He's right—I am
an undertaker for the living, consigning innocents
to birth not death, though

not every womb is warm. Let this planting
stand for all inhospitable beginnings,
for what shivers unseen awaiting its chance.

Foot to shovel, back to wind, sky dour with
coming rain, crows squawking, a few creaking pines,
the hoarse whisper of corn stalks blowing,

their dry matter to be thrown on the pile—
I could work up a good sweat of melancholy here
if wonder were not constantly interrupting.

I'm fifty. I take no comfort in the rites of religion.
Let me see the miracle before me,
the one I too am.

Let planting bring me to my knees.

LEAVINGS

—to John

By the power of dark upon the lake at dusk,
by the power of our affection,
the way you feel like home to me and I to you,
I went out
into the evening chill of air and shadow,
into trees and hills, lake and sky,
and into you, my friend, into you,
and what had seemed until then outside me
was within,
an in without an ending,
an in without an out.

From a fathomless body, dark and still,
I saw those gunwaled minds
athwart their own desires. The you and I
I thought I knew, our skin,
our beating, salty flow and spout of words
I saw as circles drawn to then erase.
You laughed right then,
a rippled laugh that spread in widening circles out
and feared no end.

Be well, my friend. We are ever near,
though life soon drags us far.

To Muffin (in memoriam)
—for Sam

One big, healthy hunk of cat you were,
strongly muscled under gray and white fur,
dusty from the barn. Crossing the lawn,
haunches rolling with a tiger's machismo,
one might wonder how *you* could be a "Muffin"—
yet you fed us daily with your joy.
For you had the right ingredients.
Eager spirit and enormous ears
dwarfed your paws at the shelter where you batted
paper clips my Sam had strung together
seeking a playmate for his playful heart,
both of you so much the same it seemed—
happy, ready for action, always outdoors,
shy with strangers, sponges for affection.
When I'd lie with Sam on his bed at bedtime,
listening for his breath to slow and settle,
you would spring from darkness without warning,
assault us with your presence, plopping between,
nuzzling our faces, leaning with exuberance
into every stroke, making the room
full with the sound of your bliss. Then you'd sleep
draped on Sam's chest, his neck, his ear—no wonde
he drew cat cartoons, made books on cats,
even did school projects on cats, for you
filled his sleep, filled his world with affection,
filled his nose with cat hair.
                              So I shattered,
organs ruptured on impact when the neighbor
brought me to your body lying limp and
flattened by the road. I carried you home,

supple and warm, holding yet some comfort.
I did not mind the bloody clothes—it was
your blood, after all, pure and holy
like the drool of children. I laid you by the
kitchen door, family filing out
to face the fact, the unalterable fact,
you were gone.

                    Never had I wept
so openly for anyone, or since.
Sam then lay alone in his bedroom darkness,
that same dark from which you nightly sprang.
Joining him we lay on the bed together
in the impotence of loss, darkness
now your presence and your absence, memory
wounder and healer both, fear the shadow
love casts.

               How could we have kept you safe,
kept you inside against your nature? How would
that have preserved you?

                    Every single morning
you would sail forth from our door
hoisting your tail as a flag of liberty,
ever full of courage, the momentum of
life itself, onward into your vast
chlorophyll sea, eager for the smells and
sights of yard and woods. You would sit
tranquilly in rapture on a post,
ablaze in sunlight, while I, at the window, would
have you with coffee for breakfast. For you knew
how to spend your precious life among us—
free of regret, free of obligation,
solely on what gave you joy.

From a Third-Floor Window

Already cars are beginning to lumber down
their designated canyons, creasing the air
with passing steel and coasting toward some

paid confinement. How unlike the birds,
boundless in their trajectories, trackless—
what they are in is without in or out.

A lone church tower penetrates the space
of their kingdom of praise above the trees,
but the congregation seldom ventures up;

they huddle in the box below, warm.
Meanwhile bright oracles lift up their voices
to fill the void. Heaven is a blue blank

that windows measure off in equal squares;
infinity in manageable pieces
enters a succession of ordinary days.

Outside, east-facing walls are growing golden
top to bottom, dormer to door, where before
only the spire reached up into the delicate

first light. Telephone poles lift wires aloft
like a consecrated chalice. Birds rest there.
Green things are starting to transubstantiate.

THE HAPPY INSOMNIAC

I do not begrudge this solitude,
bright star undimmed by other lights,
its unsought and sunless solace
at one with the animals of night
who wander afield seeking their fill.

The stuffed cranium of the study
is dark and still, and all its purposes
slumber, the inmate content to digest
a scene he scarcely recognizes
lit by the shining of distant worlds.

What a strange appetite is this!—
for absences, loss, shimmerings
beyond the failing empire of sight,
the ghostly plume of a skunk's tail
writing its scripture on the yard.

O surrounding, all-embracing Void,
accept the love of this brief life,
this ignition of ashes bellowed by breath
beneath the empty vault of your presence.
I refuse no gift of wakefulness.

THE CLEARING

—for Annie

Late September. I'm in the pasture
tearing out old rusted wire bittersweet vines ensnare.
Scores of saplings, puppies of the woods who know no bounds,
poke eagerly through, the larger already swallow the steel
in their haste to thicken and rise. The air
chilled from this morning's frost—our first—
grass soaked with the sweat of night,
I'm stripped to T-shirt,
biceps ache from squeezing loppers
that sever the hopes of young wood to be forest,
back sore from heaving bottom wire
buried in ground and hoisting the bulldog
chain saw to chew the heftier fellows through,
but there's nowhere I would rather be today
than here repairing the disregard of years,
grateful for the strength of limb and will
to push back the wood's encroachment,
getting the fence ready for the new arrival—
a horse—whose coming gives this clearing purpose.
Here is the freedom on this crisp day
to work in my own field for my daughter's dream,
to bask in the warmth of sun and a warmth within—
twin hearths of nature—
cozying up to a sense of blessing,
knowing how a mind can feel cursed with toil—
and I do sometimes curse the tenacity of trees.
But today, as a yellow light glistens on leaves
that tremble in what will soon undo them,
I know I will not always be here.

I am but a clearing between thick woods,
a brief opening where the sun enters,
of little consequence but
unspeakable worth, happy to be fodder
for the continuance of things.

NOTES

Cover: The photo is of the McTyre barn, lone structure from a former homestead. The barn is constructed of hand-hewn beams and pegs and hand-forged nails and stands on the US highway 195 between Colfax and Pullman on land formerly farmed by Don Hart and Charles Hofer.

"The Vanishing Point":

p. 18, **Shunt, etc.**—The subject of this poem suffers from hydrocephalus.

p. 19, **P-51**—a World War II bomber escort fighter airplane.

p. 19, **Three swastikas**—Allied World War II pilots would celebrate their "victories," Nazi planes they had shot down, by painting a swastika on their plane just below the cockpit.

p 19, **Palouse**—a region of eastern Washington State and Northern Idaho south of Spokane and north of the Snake River

"Flight from Duxford":

p. 24, The Don Hart quotation is from an oral account recorded in Lt. Col. R. A. "Dick" Hewitt's book, *Target of Opportunity: Tails and Contrails of The Second World War* (Cotopaxi, CO: Cosson Printing Services, 2000), p. 130. Hart's whole account may be found on pages 129-135.

"Midnight in a Pond in Lincoln, Massachusetts":

p. 50, translation of the Latin epigraph: *This thing of nature [water] does not receive us properly unless we are naked.*

MARK D. HART, born on Valentine's Day in 1956, grew up on a wheat farm in the Palouse region of eastern Washington State. He now lives in western Massachusetts, where he is a Licensed Mental Health Counselor in private practice, the guiding teacher for the Bodhisara Dharma Community, on the teaching staff of Insight Meditation Center of the Pioneer Valley, and a religious advisor at Amherst College. He holds a masters degree in counseling from Seattle University and a doctorate in theology from Boston College and has taught religious studies at both Seattle University and Smith College. He began writing poetry in 2003 after the death of his father. Since then his work has appeared in *Atlanta Review, RATTLE, Poetry East, Margie, The Midwest Quarterly, Tar River Poetry, The Spoon River Poetry Review* and numerous other journals. *Boy Singing to Cattle* is his first book of poetry.